About the Author

This collection of poems is the latest one the author has written. Previously published were 'Transforming the Moment' and 'Ending and Unending'. The poems are inspired by a regular practice of meditation as is explained in the Preface to this book.

FRAGMENTS OF HOPE

Margrit Dahm

FRAGMENTS OF HOPE

Vanguard Press

A CIP catalogue record for this title is available from the British
Library.

ISBN 978-1-83794-259-6

*Vanguard Press is an imprint of
Pegasus Elliot Mackenzie Publishers Ltd.*
www.pegasuspublishers.com

First Published in 2024

**Vanguard Press
Sheraton House Castle Park
Cambridge England**

Printed & Bound in Great Britain

PREFACE

In this collection of poems, it is my intention to put into words how a regular practice of meditation gradually changes and penetrates our life in so many different ways; the way we look at and experience nature, the way we learn to relate to others, not only to those who are like-minded, but also to those we find difficult to be with; we learn to adopt a non-judgmental attitude, we learn to be more tolerant and to endure any displeasing behaviour with a greater degree of patience. Our relationship with the divine becomes more intimate and loving, and even when we go through times of hardship, be it physical or mental, we are never completely without hope.

Our life becomes more balanced. We still have our ego we will never be without it, but because we are growing inwardly and refresh our inner resources with every meditation, the ego is learning to serve rather than to dominate, and so inner and outer can be in unison which makes us happier, more joyful and more appreciative; we truly become what we were meant to be – human beings who don't just act and react mechanically like a well-oiled machine, but where a deeper consciousness is closer at hand.

As John Main who is the founder of the Christian Meditation movement puts it:

"The important aim in Christian meditation is to allow God's mysterious and silent presence within us to become more and more not only a reality, but the reality which gives meaning, shape and purpose to everything we do, everything we are."

And recently, I stumbled across these words: "When there is true self, there is hope; and when there is hope, there is everything." It is an apt description, it seems to me, of what this particular way of life is about.

Margrit Dahm

On the Bus

The bus is rattling along the high street
and with a jerk comes to a stop:
people want to get off and get on
and the bus fills up with passengers;

all manner of noise can be heard:
the discontent crying of a baby,
the Italian natter of a couple in the back,
the boisterous manifestations of a boy,
a mobile phone starts to ring...

yet it takes only a moment
to become aware of these different
sounds, and being present to them
we enter a different dimension

where the Now, unperturbed by
the different goings-on, is enveloped,
during this short time of our journey,
in a feeling of love and compassion
toward our fellow travellers

Now

Beyond the squares of the Gothic window
a confusion of bare branches
is obscuring the sky with their starkness,

behind, in the back of the room
the hubbub of voices
is gradually fading away,

and in a brief moment
of awareness
the Now is catching up with time

Dusk

The slate roof was tinged
with pink and purple sunshine
while the sun was setting in the west;

no foliage has yet sprung up
on the old tree's knotty branches,
and the twigs hang limp
from too much rain;

but between the paleness
of a murky sky
and the receding of a ruffled day,
dusk is able to recover
some of its soft lucidity,
and presaging the approaching night,
the earth can now breathe freely

The Nightingale

When the nightingale
sings its nocturnal song
in the bushes down below,

the world surrounding it
is plunged into silence;

for nothing wants to stir
or interrupt its
still and sonorous voice;

how contained it is in the
dark fullness of the night!

And yet, its sound is
as clear as the water
rushing blithely down the
mountain side;

and when its song
has ceased at last,
its mild and mellow beauty
goes on to echo
in the heart, like the
whisper of a silent prayer

The Old Tree

The tree stood in the green for all to see:
large, substantial, grey, and of great age;
like an elephant's skin, its trunk
was embedded in furrows and wrinkles,
while its crown was far-reaching and wide.

Generations have sat in its shade,
children played in its perimeter –
mute and silent, big and strong
it has weathered the passage of time
guarding its secret in the folds of its bark

When Dawn is Breaking

When the molten mass of darkness
is broken up by the dawn's
weightless and shimmering light,

the heart is quick to respond,
and breathing freely,
it follows the trail which
leads to the soft and gentle touch

of divine love; nestling in its shade,
the oriole can be heard
singing its song

Into the Darkness

Where the light shone brightly before
is now the dim semi-darkness of twilight,

where there was the deep of the ocean
is now the misty veil of non-existence,

where there was the open space
is now the enclosure of mute dispassion:

putting its feelers out – here, there, beyond
and nowhere – darkness meets with silence,

but the soul, feeling empty and bare,
is wishing for more...

Towards

The light seems so far off,
the soul, craving for the light,
is plunged into the darkness
of its absence which is
holding her fast,
weighing her down...

a gentle hand takes hold of her
guiding her towards the light,
and she puts her trust
in the steadfastness
of the invisible cross

Through the Dark

When dark clouds
want to obscure
the chamber of the heart,

an angel of light
is urging us on
through the undefined
vapours of gloom
scattering behind him

fragments of hope

Bereft

When the heart seems heavy-laden
and full of sadness,
when joy seems to have left us
and the glimpses of divine
presence

appear to be distant and forlorn,
our call is but the echo
which reverberates among the
rocks up the mountain side

while the mantra,
as though ringing from
beneath a well,
continues to sound within
the depth of our being

The Pain...

The emotional pain
which can be inflicted by other people
ought to be borne by us without
any criticism or blame;
as it is written: 'Take your yoke upon
you and learn from me';

but it is also said: 'my yoke is easy
and my burden light'...

therefore, let's detach ourselves
from any thoughtless implications,

and the pain which we feel
will become for us a guiding force
where sorrow can be turned into love

Balance is Restored

When balance is again restored
and harmony regains its worth,

shadows are at once dispersed
as they soon give way
to a brighter, sunlit day,

and spread out like a fresh
untainted sheet on which
our tired limbs and weary
minds can come to rest,

the spirit of unclouded peace
returns to our troubled souls

and our heart can once more be
filled with gratitude and joy

Pendulum

Perpetual growth
induces strength
persistent strength
endows the meek:

perpetual love
invites the strong
to wander further
into life:

perpetual meekness
finds itself
confronted with endurance:
to endure is to grow
in love and strength and virtue

Homecoming

The window is ablaze with light,
welcoming light,
light which dispels darkness
and which by its warmth
awakens the feeling
of having arrived,
of coming home at last –

coming home from the cold
coming home from the darkness –

as we enter the room
no words are needed
to express how we feel
for we are expected

and a notion arises in us,
a notion that this is the place
for which we've searched
and which wanted to be found:
at this moment of
recognition and acceptance
our efforts are laid to rest
and we are at peace

At the Interval

As though they want to pay
homage once more to all creation
before the night finally sinks
into the deep of the earth, the birds
are busy singing their song –
their melodious, joyful, fluid song
sung with so much ease,

when the scream of
the police car's siren –
shrill and sharp, penetrating,
of man-made precision,
pierces the air

overriding momentarily
the hour of nature's interval
when the motion of the day
meets with the repose of the night
and the inner space begins to
foreshadow the language of silence

City Noises

Amidst the crowded streets,
the combustion of engines
the loud voices on their mobiles,

amidst the ever present
absent-mindedness of constant
hurry and haste,

there is the tranquil oasis
of the cultivated gardens nearby:

its joyful calm offers
rest and refreshment,

leading us back for a while
to the kind of inner peace which

had been absent, and will
leave us again, when
we continue our journey,

a journey on which we hope
to arrive at an ever increasing
awareness of that which is

Time to Be

The sea of unknowing
is in and around us;
it allows the heart

to glide on its swell
and with a touch lighter
than light, it lets

our being breathe
freely in the breeze,

and little ripples
move playfully across

the surface of the water

while the deep is filled
with life-giving silence

The Month of May

How joyous are the sounds of spring
when life is born in great abundance:

the trees are dressing their leafy crowns,
the wind is caressing the opening bloom,

the birds are calling wanting to mate
and sunrays are falling from brighter skies,

the days are ruling with prolonged cheer
and the nights retreat into later hours –

inspired by nature,
we welcome the change
from conspicuous bleakness
to the richness of life,

and being aware
of the transforming grace
in and around us

we are taking delight
in inner resources
and the feast of the eye

A New Season

When in spring the trees
are green with tender leaves,

when the swifts possess the skies,

when the days are getting
longer by the hour,
and the sun acclaims
the great outdoors,

when we shake of
winter's slackness,

and hidden secrets in the garden
quietly reverberate with joy,

we are as if immersed
in rising forces

where the undulating tide
of the approaching summer
anticipates its rich
and lavish leniency,

and entering through
the hidden gate,
we leave the winter months
behind at last

Beginning and End

The cry of the raven
which is heard, but not seen,
sounding lost and forlorn,
trails away in the stillness

which has fallen upon
the sunny garden paths,
midway between
morning and night

calling to mind
the hours already spent
and the time
which is yet to come

in order to make
this day complete
in its beginning and end

Sounds on a Summer's Day

The ether is full of vibrations and sounds
which echo in the sun-drenched air on
this clear and cloudless summer's day.

Closer nearby, the birds are clamouring
in the garden and the bees hum around
the sweet smelling heads of lavender.

On the terrace, under the sunshade,
people have gathered round the table;

the soft murmur of voices evokes
the sensation that this is a day which
wants to be lived and witnessed
fully and joyfully in the here and now

There Is

There is something comforting
in the perennial themes of life –
the heartbeat which keeps
everything alive, is moving forward
at its appropriate speed:

the regularity of the four seasons
invoke in us a sense
of steadiness and constancy,

and we welcome the different
events and celebrations
which are connected with them
and occur throughout the year;
they give us the assurance

that we matter
and that people matter,
that we give
as well as receive
by being part of them,

and by not obstructing the
change which is inherent

31

in all things temporal,
we become more fully aware
of that which always is

Attentiveness

Call it charity, compassion or love:
it is this force which alone knows
how to tame the endless flow
of restless drifting thoughts,

when we enter at last that
inner space which is waiting,

and with the arrival
of this timeless moment our
human task is complete and done

Our Cosmos

The inner room is full of joy
and music echoes through its space,
whatever benchmark you employ
it never ceases to amaze.

Here, every blade of grass is known,
accounted for each grain of sand,
every piece of rock and every stone
are wondrous things to comprehend:

Take a feather, so weightless, light
how intricate is its design,
it may be black, just grey or white
or its colours may gleam and shine –

the outer world in many ways befits
the inner world with all its secrets,
and within the cosmos in which we live
is surely much to learn and much to give

A New Vision

Let every wound be wrapped
in a healing veil,
let memories float away
on the crest of the ocean,
let the pervading power of love
sink deep into your heart –
let peace prevail,

and in following the trail
things will begin
to change in your
life and in yourself:
mark each moment
as a new endeavour –
let peace prevail,

let a steady wind fill your sail,
make room in your cabin,
and the spirit's breath
will enter in;
feel its strength at every
step and marvel at
its surprising fruitful action –
let peace prevail

Listening

Listen to the words
which were spoken for you to hear,
and let their meaning
float into your heart;

here, they will find the source
which will transform them
into compassion and understanding;

thus, your listening ear and
kindly words
may be able to bring comfort

to those who turned to you
at a time of need or simply wanted
to share with you their joy

A Moment in Time

An evening in late August:
the light is still profuse,
and a breeze which, having lost
all humidity, is refreshingly
cool after the rain.

There is a feeling
of serenity and calm
in this early evening hour which
seems to inhabit the indoor
as well as the outdoor life –

there are no noises nor other
disturbances or distractions,
only the playful display of
light and shadow,
the tantalisingly lyrical
whisper of the leaves,

as well as the overture of the
setting sun when the day
gives way to the twilight zone

where the boundaries

of the temporal world
meet with the open
blue sphere of the Eternal

Late at Night

The shimmer of a waxing moon
has touched the interior
of the room with its soft and
reticent light –

being unobtrusively restful,
it is not meant to illuminate
or shine, but to embellish
the darkness of a clear night;

unlike the electric light
which immediately sharpens
the contours inside and out

and unlike the sunlight
which brightens the day
infusing colour into the world
of nature and man,

it does not aim at
penetrating the dark, but
simply at rendering the night
more mysterious with
its glistening stillness
and silent gleams

Two Worlds –

The visible and the invisible:
one is our earthly life with all its
boundaries and limitations,
its finality being measured
within the realm of time –

the other is like a ray of sun
when it is mirrored
a hundredfold
in the raindrop on the petal
of a rose from where
it is sending forth starry lights,

while the universe beholds
its luminous darkness
where the heavenly bodies
know no bound as they
perform their dance within
the ethereal space of infinity

Then and Now

Back in the same room with the
Gothic window, the mind remembers:

last time: the dark branches of the trees
outside being silhouetted against a cloudless
sky, had been bared by the cold of winter,

this time, they are still covered
with late summer's foliage –

memory pointing to the past and
the experience of the now,

time within time
where the changing and unchanging
are both equally present,

when the moving and unmoving
are both contained in the still point

foreshadowing the way to time future
and retaining it at the same time...

About Attention

What we call attention
is something so intangible
and elusive when we consider
how short the timespan is
that can keep us focused
on one thing without turning
to another in our thoughts;

but if we add love
to this state of collectiveness,
we will see and listen
with our hearts;
we will be ready when
this loving attention is
freely given,

and it will draw us
deeper into the mystery
of that other reality
where we will always be
beginners learning
to give and to receive
learning to respond,
learning to be...

Reality

Love makes all travail
lighter, rendering it durable
and beneficial for the soul:

it purifies the intentions
of the heart and offers healing
to those ills and pains which
ask for our forbearance;

when we so discern at last
that we are loved as we are
inclined to love in return

we encounter Reality
for the first time, and are
amazed at the intrinsic
power of its beauty

Twilight

Breathe in the peace
of the evening hour,
breathe in the sunshine
of the setting sun

and while the birds
find their resting place,
let the loving sound
of your sacred word

resound in the depths
of your being
greeting the approaching
night with a gesture

of ready approval,
and letting go of the day,
you'll recognize
the joy dwelling within

Within, Without

Without a sound and
with great gentleness,
like in a mild and soft caress
the falling rain is touching

the earth which
in turn receives and retains it
eagerly drinking in
the refreshing balm;

the air is so very still and calm –
no gust of wind
nor the fairest breeze
can be felt within, without

while out of the cloud
the raindrops fall,
fall till the rain will cease...

Aspects of Time

What was felt yesterday
with such intensity
has become today
a matter of unconcern

and will have turned
tomorrow into something
of utter insignificance

On Your Way

Let the morning star
rise in your heart
when you get up and
when you sit down;

then humbly acknowledge
and recognize the precious
gift which you are given

each time you fold your
hands in silent prayer and
loving faithfulness;

for what is bestowed
echoes in the joy you feel
and the devotion
you return to –

let the morning star
rise in your heart and
guide you on your way

In the Now

Open the door to the future
by dwelling in the present moment,

for in such unifying
consciousness
all elements of time are
contained simultaneously,
without separation,
without division –

and all manner of things
will be one when we
can take rest in the
purifying awareness
of his divine presence

Morning is Rising

The mist of dawn
was hanging like
grey flannel sheets
between the trees,

and the air,
moist and scented,
was rising from the ground,

until the moment when
the first sunrays were
infusing light into the
greyness of the
early morning scene –

immediately, colour
was restored
and the sharp outlines
of another day procured

Rain

Rain, silent rain,
falling from heaven
and drenching the ground
with its beneficial
blissfulness.

Hardly seen,
but eagerly received,
its fall is a gift
which helps to maintain
the balance of fruitfulness
above and below.

Never foreseen,
but often sensed, it
contains the prospect
of abundant harvesting
which shares its plenitude
with the welfare of man

Insight

A true insight is something
that is not just understood
by the head alone,

but with our whole being;
for it is experienced
in and through the
innermost part of our heart

The Community

When love begins to grow in us
and joy gets hold of every fibre,
self-love has less room in us,

and we let go of selfish thinking;

instead we pray and work together,
we consider each other's welfare
and keep in mind the need of others

when we return to our daily lives;

many are those who do not have
the blessing of that guiding grace
and seek to be enlightened

in the way of godliness;

but to those who do not want to
hear our voice, we lend a listening ear,
for many are their grievances

which might contain a question;

so let us be part of the community
and let us welcome every stranger
who seeks our help in many a way,

let us be their manger

Autumn Haze

The dimmed light of autumn
was cast over the sky
diminishing the openness
of summer when all was bright
and full of life's vitality;

in place of bloom and growth
there is now withdrawal:
the fading away, the waning
and wasting,

and yet, we know
that the force which animates
all living things
will not die,

but temporarily out
of reach, it is preserved
in the hidden depths
of the earth,

only to be revived
when the time is ripe,

we know that the
immanent breath of life
is there for us
to be redefined

Falling Leaves

Soundlessly, but abundantly,
calling to mind
the swift movement
of detachment and
transcendence,

the leaves, no longer clinging
to the branches,
tumble down to the ground,
weightless, withered, worn –

and the ground becomes
the canvas for nature's
colourful palette

Return

Autumn came and went
in October's flame
while all the summers sent
their farewell;

the sun was for ever kindling
the blue relish
of the horizon's expanding
and unwinding path

which had filled the earth
with longing, and arresting,
she withdrew
into the cool returning
current of restful calm –

short are now the hours
of awakening,
long will be the waiting
for another spring

Step Out

Step out into the cold
and feel your fingers
go numb and stiff
and walk on –

do not forget the woman
by the wayside
who receives the alms
of mercy –

and walk on
in order to receive
your share
of the heavenly bread

Steps

To take an inner step
can take a long time
or perhaps
it never happens

or perhaps we are
not aware
of the fact
that it has happened

meanwhile,
we step in and out
of our doors
all the time

Tolerance

Can we be loving
to those who,
unlike us, are not
bent on
things of the spirit?

Do we not judge them
when their mind is set
on material things?

But are we not also
affected by
the material world
around us?
Where therefore is
the difference? –

Unless there is
no difference:
On closer inspection,
they may become us, as we
may become them,
on different occasions,
and we are always
connected by the
one who made us all

Restored

After the storm
the reconciliation:
sun meeting earth again,
earth finding its rhythm
once more
between light and darkness,
between stillness and
movement,

and in the calmness
which follows
is reflected
the all-pervading breath
of nature and man,
of creation and created,

and equilibrium has
been restored once more

Those Moments

When every trace of courage
seems to have vanished,
and the world seems nothing
but an empty, hostile place,

when friends are far away
and empathy is rare to find,

a prayer, rising from the heart
and gradually ascending
to the height of unknown skies,

begins to reaffirm what
had been there before,
and redefining the notions
of trust and hopefulness,

confidence is felt once more

The Wonder of Life

A flower, plant or budding shrub,
clothed in their own beauty,
an animal or the stature of a man
which was created with
both eyes and ears,
and hands and feet,

the sun and stars forever orbiting
in endless spaces –

we cannot really comprehend
Infinity or the richness of creation;

whatever man has achieved or made
will always be a pale reflection
of this great and wondrous world;

but there is also a connection which
lets us touch the heavenly sphere,
for the Incarnation has set us free
to follow the path laid out for us,

and reaching out, we find the way
to find the Word within the world
and the shining light thereof

He Who Is

Like the needle to a magnet,
we are drawn to
the beauty of the Eternal,

as long as our hearts are
open and receptive,

and through the gentle power
of love we begin to experience
the proximity of he who is

Advent

In the twilight of our lack of
knowledge and understanding
and the thicket
of our rambling thoughts

a searchlight
is feeling its way forward
towards some
firmer ground
where we can patiently wait

for the morning star
to rise in our hearts,
leaving us with the promise

that dawn will break
and we will see the light

symbolised in the candle
burning on the advent wreath

Communion

I am bigger and greater
than your different thoughts,
plans and desires;

with my love
I draw you ever closer
to my generous heart;

while my spirit
descends on you
with the light touch
of morning dew,

the gentle energy of life
makes my longing for you
known to you,

and when the days'
activities finally get hold
of you,

your different thoughts,
plans and desires
are watched and guided by
my unswerving wakefulness

The Christmas Miracle

Who designed the bands of
festive street lights in the High Street
providing such joyful illumination,

who decorated
the shop windows and gave them
Christmas cheer?

Inside, the shops display
their wares to offer us ideas
for Christmas gifts and presents;

be it big or small and insignificant,
commercialised or visualised,
the message seeps through
all these outward signs:

it is the wish that once a year
we want to forget about ourselves
and seek instead the other you;

thus, to celebrate in all its ways
the precious gift of human love

67

which is protected by that greater
love, the light which transforms us all

In Anticipation of Christmas

Are we ready and prepared
for the heavenly king's arrival?
Have we swept the floor
and gathered up the remnants
of our disorderly emotions
and desires?

Have we cleared the neglected
corners of our untidy minds and
instead adorned it with the
decorous flower of humility
and the scent of selflessness?

When we have thus worked
and laboured in readiness
of his coming, we will find

that he rather chose
the little cradle of our
innermost self –

from there to send forth
his radiant light
filling the room with his

abundant gift of love and joy,

and holding our attention
on the source of such
splendour,

we recognize,
perhaps for the first time,
that our wish to be
is a reality which is waiting
to be embraced

Love

Who has not dwelled on the past?
Who has not planned for the future?
But between past and future
there rests the present moment –
the timespan in which humanity is born

The Dance

the firmament was dimmed
in order to dislodge
the millions of heavenly bodies
hidden therein.

Meeting the horizon,
they multiplied in numbers
and gained in volume,
enchanted, they beheld
the heavens above,

and rising, they encountered brightness,
moving, they began to dance,

and forming circles upon circles,
they gathered round beyond the spheres,

and filled the air with sounds of
music in adoration, praise and joy

A Prayer

Be the centre of my life
Be my peace and be my strife
Be the first of morning's duty
Be the last when sleep forsakes me

Be the voice before it's heard
Be the sense in every word
Be the silence yet unstirred
Be the song of every bird

Be the spark in someone's eyes
Be the light of unknown skies
Be the shade beneath the tree
Be the darkness rendered free

Be the hand to ease the fall
Be my centre, be my all

Signs of Life

The raven,
carrying a twig
in its beak,
alights for a brief
moment on the
bare branch of
the maple tree,

before it spreads
its wings to fly away
into the future,

leaving behind
the promise of
new life and
a new spring

The Eternal Spring

When the abundance
of the eternal spring
begins to fill our heart,

we no longer dwell
in the twilight
of much indecision

where yes and no
are constantly debated,

but instead, a step of

confidence and trust
carries us swiftly
forward into

the Here and Now

How

How big and wide your heart must be
forever to embrace humanity;

how great must be your tolerance
to so endure man's violence;

how deep must your wisdom be
to uphold and lift our integrity;

how strong your love for us must be
to be revealed in its immensity

in the son who came to earth
to teach us and proclaim your worth

A Bond

When true compassion
meets with the kind of love
we have to offer,

a bond is created,
a connection made

which is tangible,
enduring and unifying

A World Within

When I enter into the sanctuary,
I leave my dusty shoes behind,
I step forward silently
and let mind and thoughts unwind;

brightened by the soft and calming light,
the space within begins to open wide,
I am welcomed in and I rejoice
while listening to the gentle voice;

in this company I stay
till daily tasks call me away,
but I know I can return
and the light won't cease to burn

Please!

Let me find
refuge
in your strength,
solace
in your magnitude,
mirth
in your eternal beauty,
freedom
in your living will,
protection
in your wakefulness,
courage
in your reign of justice,
tranquillity
in your gentleness,

and may your guidance
never fail
to let me recognize
you in my soul

Let It Be So

Let the overwhelming joy
we feel drive away all
interfering, needless thoughts,

let the gracious love which
you placed into our hearts
supersede all selfish notions,

let the light of your gentle
presence dispel the obscurity
of our frequent inequity,

let your continued grace
restore in us the kind of
innocence we used to have,

and let the peace of your
boundless mercy replace all
hostility and fretfulness

Each Day

With faith being our guide,
love being the driving force,
and hope sustaining our efforts,

we regard each day
as a new beginning
and a new opportunity,

and each day finds its
completion in the
incompleteness of our prayer

Poverty of Spirit

Gently, the door is opened
and the silence which awaits us
takes hold of our being:

light pours into our hearts,
and we experience the freedom
of the poor in spirit

As Though

As though we were
touching the edge of
his garment,

his healing power
sinks deep into
our heart

which will then
express itself
in works of love

I Am

We step into the inner room:
the presence of it is such
that we soon leave
the outside world behind,

and we focus on the silence:
the sound of our sacred word
echoes through the space

until the outer person, too,
is fully alive and attentive,

and the wholeness of our
being which we experience
allows us then to say:

I Am Here Now

Home Is...

Home is where the heart is:
if it is set on greed and competition,
it loses its internal vision
and something is amiss;

but when the heart is keeping watch
and welcomes the spirit in,
mind and heart can then begin
to be a perfect match:

the mind takes up its leading role,
the heart can then breathe freely,
and remembering our final goal,
we accept our gift most gratefully

Not Yet

It seems we have to be
reconciled with ourselves
first before we can
resolve differences with
someone else,

but let's not be surprised
if this someone is not yet
prepared to let go
of opinions and viewpoints:

we have to be ready
for a change of heart...

It Is…

It is not by making the mind
'blank' that we meditate,
as some people suggest,

but it is the peace
which arises from inside
and begins to fill both mind

and body which bring about
the change, for within
this peace dwells life itself

Words and Silence

Can you sit together with a friend
without words and in peaceful silence
and not be embarrassed or defend
your mind's truly tranquil moments?

There is a silence which can speak
more than any words can do
in which you rest, but also seek
the other person and the other you,

and when you talk again at leisure,
it is as though you always knew
that only both in such equal measure
portray a friendship to be true

Affirmation

The last sounds
of the Matthew Passion
have just passed away;

we were silent,
and the silence spread
like an unspoken pledge
from one person to the next;

calm and tranquillity descended,
and I experienced
the affirmation
of the simple truth:

where two or three
are gathered in my name,
I am right among them...

And So They Walk On...

The children of light
who walk in the shadow
of he who is,
do not fear

the approaching hurdle
which awaits them
at the end of the passage
through which
they must pass

where friction wants
to raise its head,

where effort is
the food of life,

and where joy
and sorrow are
closely connected:

then light will become darkness
and darkness will turn into light,
joy will engulf sorrow

and sorrow will be their joy,

and so they walk on,
the children of light,
and nothing will harm them
on their wondrous journey
from which they will not return

The Morning Star

Wait until the morning star will rise
and it will guide you to the light,
wait until love comes to abide
in your heart, and it will make you wise;

without the light we cease to be,
without the light we're bound to flee
into life's persistent strife
which takes away internal life;

but when the morning star begins to shine,
all worldly things will intertwine,
all measure of things will come to be
in the Lord's tender care eternally

In My Father's House

There is a chamber to which we can withdraw,
to which a different reality applies:
we enter in through the most secret door
and are surprised about its size;

it is at once both big and small
and is astoundingly construed,
it is not marked by any wall,
and yet is spacious, wide and tall;

it is well hidden from the naked eye,
but by those who seek it will be found,
and those who knock will by and by
find access to its sacred ground;

here time stands still without regret,
and space defines a new dimension,
not on desire here the heart is set
as it takes up its humble station –

in my father's house are many places,
and this is one which we have found;
it reverberates and it embraces
all music with its most gentle sound